Adoption

Questions and Feelings About . . .

PICTURE WINDOW BOOKS
a capstone imprint

by Anita Ganeri
illustrated by Ximena Jeria

Questions and Feelings About ... is published by
Picture Window Books, a Capstone imprint
1710 Roe Crest Drive, North Mankato, MN 56003
www.mycapstone.com

U.S. edition copyright © 2020 by Picture Window Books, a Capstone Imprint

Library of Congress Cataloging-in-Publication Data is available on
the Library of Congress website.

ISBN: 978-1-5158-4539-3 (library binding)

Editor: Melanie Palmer
Design: Lisa Peacock
Author: Anita Ganeri
Consultant: Jo Mitchell

First published in Great Britain in 2018
by The Watts Publishing Group
Copyright © The Watts Publishing Group, 2018
All rights reserved.

Printed and bound in China.
001593

Adoption

Being part of a family is special. You care for each other. You have fun together. You argue with each other. You make up.

Your parents look after you as you grow up.
They help keep you safe.

How does it feel
to be part of
your family?

There are many ways of making a family. Some families have a mom and a dad. Some have two moms or two dads. Some have just one parent.

Sometimes parents can't live together and they split up. They might find other partners. Then you might have a stepmom or a stepdad.

Who is in your family?

The family you're born into is called your birth family. Sometimes children cannot live with their birth families.

This might be because their birth parents are ill or finding it hard to look after themselves. They cannot look after the children or keep them safe.

If children can't live with their birth families, they may be adopted. This means that they go to live with a new family.

Some children are adopted when they're babies. Some are adopted when they're older. Some children are adopted with their brothers or sisters.

Social workers are people who look for a new family. They visit the family at home and meet the mom and dad. They also meet any family pets.

They come back for a lot more visits. They ask the family lots of questions to make sure that it will be the right family for the child.

Some children live with a foster family until they can go to their new family. They may stay for a few months or, sometimes, a few years.

The foster family may have other children staying with them. They may have their own children living with them, too.

The big day comes when the child meets his or her new family. This might be just for a few hours or a day at first. This helps everyone get to know each other.

Meeting a new family can be exciting but scary.
The child and the new mom and dad might feel
very shy.

If everything goes well, the child moves into the new family's house. He or she may have a new bedroom to put their things in. This helps the child to feel at home.

What makes you feel at home?

Later, when the child has settled in, it is time to meet other members of the family.

Starting at a new school can feel scary.
It can feel hard to try to make new friends.

*How did you feel when
you started school?*

School friends may wonder what being adopted means. They may ask questions that the child isn't able to answer.

Being adopted can feel confusing. It can be hard for children to understand why they can't live with their birth parents.

Children who are adopted as babies may not remember their birth parents. If they are older, they may not have happy memories.

What makes you feel confused?

Children might wonder why their new family wanted to adopt them.

Their new mom might say that she couldn't grow a baby in her tummy. She wanted to adopt a child because she wanted to have a family.

Some adopted children are given a book with their life story in it. There might be photos of their birth family in the book.

The children can look through the book with their forever family. It can help them understand why they were adopted.

It's important to know who you are and where you came from. It's important to feel proud of who you are.

What would you say or do to cheer someone up?

Being adopted means being part of a family that loves you and keeps you safe. That's something to feel proud of, too.

Notes for Caregivers

This book can be a useful way for families and professionals to begin a discussion with children about what it means to be adopted. Adopted children may feel shy or vulnerable in a group situation, so it is important to be as inclusive as possible. Choice of appropriate vocabulary when discussing adoption is important. For example, rather than using the term "real parents," use "first parents," "biological parents," or "birth parents," and avoid any generalizations.

Sometimes children may be given projects at school that involve details of their family life, such as creating family trees, discussing family pictures, bringing in baby pictures, or making timelines. For an adopted child, many of these may cause them to feel left out and uncomfortable, so it is good to have a strategy for broader activities such as those mentioned on page 31.

Adoptive children may require extra support at any stage of their childhood, so it is important they are able to identify someone they can trust and talk to safely. It could be an adult, friend, or an organization that can provide support and understanding. Teaching about empathy, the diveristy of family life, and the varied types of a family will help equip children understand there are many similarities, as well as differences, between them all.

Group Activities

1. Ask the children to create a "Who's in My World?" drawing. It can include any significant people, not just direct relations. It might include family friends, teachers, community members, babysitters, pets, and so on. You could discuss how families are often made up of many people who aren't always blood relations.

2. Conduct a survey by asking the children to pinpoint one significant moment in their life development. It could be riding a bike for the first time, learning to swim, discovering a new place, tasting something amazing, or anything else that they feel was significant to them. It could be something from school or a school trip. Then create a picture chart of all the answers to show the variety of things that shape their lives, ensuring no one is excluded.

3. Read a picture book that features adoption as a theme. It is a good way to introduce the topic to a class. It could also be used as a starting point to then ask children to create their own story about someone being adopted, which would encourage and develop empathy.

Read More:

Harris, Robie H. *Who's in My Family? All About Our Families (Let's Talk about You and Me)*. Candlewick, 2012.

Kotb, Hoda. *I've Loved You Since Forever*. HarperCollins, 2018.

Schutte, Sarah L. *Adoptive Families*. Capstone Press, 2010.

Read the entire Questions and Feelings About . . . series:

Adoption
Autism
Bullying
Having a Disability
Racism
When Parents Separate
When Someone Dies
Worries